Contents

Chapter 1

AGRICULTURAL POLLUTION

Where does food come from? Many people would say it comes from the supermarket. Others might say it comes from a restaurant. But long before food gets to supermarkets and restaurants, it is produced by agriculture.

Most Americans get their food from grocery stores. Where does this food actually come from?

Agriculture is another word for *farming*. It is the process of growing plants or raising animals for food. Your morning milk and cereal, your burger at lunch, and the carrots on your dinner plate all exist because of agriculture.

▲ CEREAL IS USUALLY MADE FROM GRAINS SUCH AS OATS, CORN, OR RICE.

There are more than four million tractors in the United States.

Agriculture has been around for thousands of years. But in the 1940s, farming began to change. Farm machines, such as tractors, made it easier to plant and harvest. New methods of caring for animals meant a single farm could raise more cows, pigs, chickens, or fish. These and other changes helped farmers produce more food than ever before.

But modern farming also produces pollution. There are three main types of agricultural pollution. The first is water pollution. This happens when rainwater carries away the chemicals in farmers' fields. The second is air pollution. This occurs when livestock release gases into the atmosphere. The third type is biological pollution. This happens when fish escape from seafood farms and enter new habitats.

These pens hold fish on a fish farm. Fish farmers know it is impossible to completely prevent escapes.

Water, air, wildlife, and farmworkers are all affected by agricultural pollution. So are the foods we eat every day. But as you will see, there are things we can do to fix these problems.

Many bees have died since 2005. Scientists think one of the causes may be agricultural pollution.

Chapter 2

WATER POLLUTION

Just as people do, plants need food to grow. Plant food is called fertilizer. It is a mixture of nutrients plants need. Natural fertilizers include animal waste or compost. But most farmers use human-made chemical fertilizers. Farmers spread the chemicals on their fields. Plants take in the nutrients through their roots.

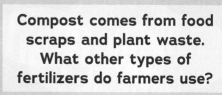

Compost comes from food scraps and plant waste. What other types of fertilizers do farmers use?

But not all of the fertilizer is taken up by plants. Some of it dissolves in rainwater. This water runs off the fields. It goes into nearby lakes and rivers. Water plants, such as algae, also eat fertilizer.

Algae have grown quickly in this lake, thanks to extra nutrients from fertilizer in the water.

Pesticides are another source of water pollution. These chemicals kill the weeds, germs, and insects that harm crops. In the United States alone, farmers spray more than one billion pounds (454 million kilograms) of pesticides on their crops each year. During spraying, droplets of pesticide are carried off by wind. Later, these droplets fall into lakes and rivers. Pesticides also run off the land into nearby bodies of water.

In the United States, 85 percent of farmland gets sprayed with pesticides.

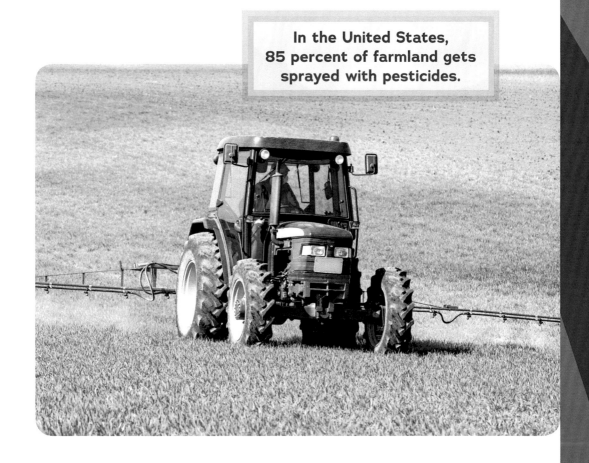

GULF OF MEXICO DEAD ZONE

Louisiana

GULF OF MEXICO

■ dead zone

Effects of Water Pollution

With extra nutrients from fertilizer, algae grows out of control. It forms thick mats on the surface of the water. The mats block sunlight. They also use up oxygen that fish need to breathe. This process is called eutrophication. It creates areas called dead zones where other plants and animals cannot live. One dead zone in the Gulf of Mexico covers more than 3,800 square miles (10,000 square kilometers). That is an area bigger than Delaware.

Pesticides in water are taken up by insects, frogs, and fish. These pesticides get stored in the animals' body fat. When predators eat these animals, they also eat the stored pesticides. Large amounts of pesticides build up inside predators. This buildup is called biomagnification. It can kill wild animals. In the 1960s, American bald eagles almost died out due to biomagnification of the pesticide DDT.

PESTICIDES ARE VERY HARMFUL TO FROGS, WHICH TAKE UP CHEMICALS THROUGH THEIR SKIN.

Even in small amounts, pesticides can cause health problems. For example, farmers who handle pesticides have higher chances of getting cancer than people who do not work in agriculture. Pesticides can also harm people who drink polluted water or eat fish from polluted lakes.

Some farmworkers wear protective suits when handling pesticides.

These bean plants add nutrients to the soil, so the next year's crop will need less fertilizer.

Solutions to Water Pollution

Farmers want to reduce the problems caused by fertilizers and pesticides. They are trying to raise crops using fewer chemicals. Crop rotation is one way to do this. Farmers plant corn one year. The next year, they plant beans. Bean plants act as a natural fertilizer and add nutrients back into the soil. As a bonus, insects that eat corn do not eat beans. While beans are growing, corn-eating insects die out.

Even with crop rotation, fertilizers and pesticides are sometimes necessary. But farmers can use less by spraying chemicals only when they are most needed. Farmers also reduce pollution by spraying only when there is no chance of wind or rain.

Small planes are used to spray pesticides and fertilizers on fields.

Chapter 3

AIR POLLUTION

In the United States, animals raised for agriculture produce nearly four times more waste than all the people in the country produce. Livestock farmers store the animals' urine and manure in containers called lagoons. One lagoon can be as big as several football fields.

A dairy farm has a large lagoon filled with waste from cows. How much waste do animals produce compared to people?

When stored waste breaks down, it releases gases into the air. For example, pig waste makes huge amounts of the gas ammonia. Animal waste also releases carbon dioxide, methane, and nitrous oxide.

ANIMALS ALSO RELEASE METHANE
WHEN THEY BURP.

Many farmers have special vehicles that spread manure on crops.

Some crop farmers use animal waste as a natural fertilizer. When spread on the surface of the soil, manure keeps breaking down. This releases more gases.

One pig produces 2.5 times more waste each day than an adult human does.

Air Pollution Effects

Ammonia smells awful. It is also dangerous to breathe. People living near pig farms often have headaches, nausea, asthma, or other health problems.

Carbon dioxide, methane, and nitrous oxide are greenhouse gases. These gases trap the sun's heat inside Earth's atmosphere. This causes the atmosphere to get warmer, just like the air inside a greenhouse. Greenhouse gases are a main cause of climate change.

Livestock produce 18 percent of all greenhouse gases released worldwide.

The gases that livestock farms produce have different effects on the atmosphere. Methane traps 34 times more heat than carbon dioxide does. Nitrous oxide traps 298 times more heat than carbon dioxide does! More and more farmers are storing animal waste in lagoons. Because of this, 54 percent more methane and nitrous oxide was produced in 2013 than in 1990. More of these powerful gases means faster climate change.

Climate change causes many problems, including the melting of ice in Earth's polar regions.

In some countries, such as Sweden, gases from animal waste are used to fuel buses.

Air Pollution Solutions

Some livestock farmers use machines to capture gases from their storage lagoons. Instead of going straight into the air, the gas is burned to make energy. This is known as biogas. Burning biogas changes the methane into carbon dioxide, a weaker greenhouse gas. This reduces air pollution from agriculture. Energy from biogas can also replace energy made by burning fossil fuels. Less use of fossil fuels helps reduce air pollution too.

Some crop farmers squirt animal fertilizer into the soil instead of spreading it over the land. This prevents gases from escaping into the air. It also reduces the chance of water pollution from runoff.

A manure injector pushes animal waste through tubes and directly into the ground.

Chapter 4

BIOLOGICAL POLLUTION

Aquaculture, or water farming, is the fastest-growing type of agriculture in the world. These farms produce fish, shrimp, and shellfish. One-third of all seafood people eat is raised on farms. Farmers raise freshwater fish in wetlands or tanks. Saltwater farming happens inside cages that separate the farm from the rest of the ocean.

These fish are being raised in tanks. Where else do people raise fish?

This fish farm in the Black Sea has high walls to prevent fish from jumping out.

Some farmers raise species that do not normally live in the waters near the farm. They bring these animals to their farms from other places in the world. But farm fish sometimes escape into the wild. Escaped fish are called alien species because they are entering a new habitat. In the wild, they are a type of biological pollution.

Why Is Biological Pollution a Problem?

Some alien species are very good at hunting. They eat a lot of small prey. This reduces the amount of food available to wild fish. Alien species may eat wild fish too. Both types of hunting can cause wild species to die out.

Escaped North American rainbow trout caused wild fish in Africa, Australia, and South America to die out.

Some farm fish also carry disease-causing germs. These germs are often harmless to alien species. But they can kill wild fish.

TOP COUNTRIES FOR AQUACULTURE PRODUCTION

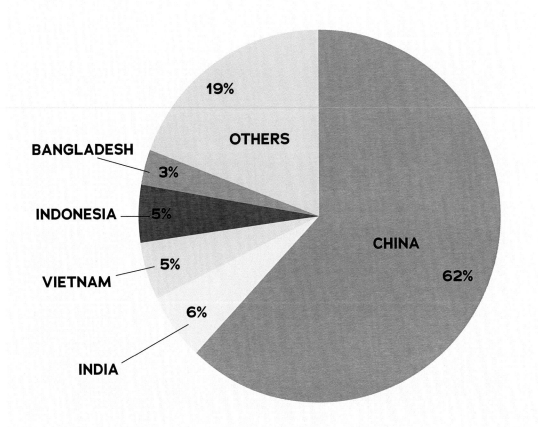

What Can We Do about Biological Pollution?

Scientists do not always know how biological pollution will affect wild animals or habitats. Because of this, strict rules control whether farmers can raise alien species. Farmers also try to keep their fish germ-free. One way is to raise fewer fish on the farm. If fish have more space, they have less chance of carrying germs. When germ-free fish escape the farm, they will not spread diseases to wild fish living nearby.

Some farmers reduce pollution by raising several species at once. For example, fish produce waste, but mussels use this waste for food.

Chapter 5

THINGS YOU CAN DO

To reduce agricultural pollution, many farmers are returning to older methods of producing food. They raise fewer animals in more space. They rotate their crops between harvests. They fertilize with natural animal or fish waste instead of chemical fertilizers.

Free-range chickens have much more space than chickens in cages. What other methods are farmers using to reduce agricultural pollution?

Farmers also find natural ways to kill pests. For instance, they add ladybugs to their fields. The ladybugs eat the insects that eat the crops. These farmers hope to produce food in a way that does not harm our environment. This is called sustainable agriculture.

LADYBUGS AND OTHER INSECTS THAT KILL PESTS ARE KNOWN AS BENEFICIAL INSECTS.

You can support these farmers by eating foods labeled *organic*. You can also look for foods labeled *free range* or *sustainably grown*. Look for these foods in supermarkets or at your local farmers' market.

Foods with organic labels have to meet strict guidelines set by the government.

Growing your own food is much cheaper than buying food at the grocery store.

Organic foods often cost more than nonorganic foods. If you cannot eat them every day, you can still help reduce agricultural pollution. Try growing food plants at home or in a community garden. And always wash fruits and veggies before eating. This removes pesticides on their skins.

Eating locally grown food also reduces pollution. To get from farm to plate, food travels in trucks that burn fossil fuels. Local food travels shorter distances than food grown farther away. Trucks that drive short distances use less fossil fuel.

Farmers' markets are great places to find local food.

Talk to your teachers or principal to see if your school's food is grown nearby.

If your school has a lunch program, find out where the food comes from. In some places, local farmers sell fresh fruits and veggies to schools. This gives kids more healthful lunches.

Finally, call or write to your government officials. Ask them to pass laws that reduce agricultural pollution. Ask them to create programs that support sustainable agriculture.

When contacting government officials, be polite. Keep writing until you get an answer.

Talk to your friends and neighbors about agricultural pollution. You can help them make choices that are better for the environment!

Remember, what happens on farms affects more than farmers. It affects our environment. It also affects the safety of the foods we eat. If we work together, we can reduce agricultural pollution!

Glossary

asthma: a disease of the respiratory system. Symptoms include wheezing, coughing, and shortness of breath.

biogas: a mixture of gases that can be burned for energy

climate change: a global change in weather patterns, including warmer temperatures, that is caused in part by greenhouse gases

compost: dead plant matter that is high in nutrients

crop rotation: growing a different crop in the same field each year to keep the soil healthy and reduce insect pests

fossil fuel: a source of energy that comes from plants and animals that died long ago. Coal is one type of fossil fuel.

habitat: the place where a plant or animal normally lives

livestock: animals raised on farms for their meat, milk, or eggs

nutrient: a substance or chemical that living things must eat or take up to survive

organic: foods that were grown without chemical fertilizers or pesticides

pesticide: a chemical used to kill weeds, insects, or diseases that harm plant crops

species: a group of living things that are all the same type

wetland: a wild habitat where a lot of water is naturally found in the soil

Learn More about Agricultural Pollution

Books

Flounders, Anne. *Growing Good Food.* South Egremont, MA: Red Chair Press, 2014. This book explores how the foods we choose to buy can have big effects on the environment.

Levete, Sarah. *Toxins in the Food Chain.* New York: Crabtree, 2010. This fascinating book helps readers understand the problems that pollution causes to our food supply.

Rodger, Ellen. *Reducing Your Foodprint: Farming, Cooking, and Eating for a Healthy Planet.* New York: Crabtree, 2010. Rodger provides lots of great ideas for reducing the harmful environmental effects of food production.

Websites

Agriculture in the Classroom
http://www.agclassroom.org/kids/index.htm
Learn more about agriculture through interactive games and activities.

Sci4Kids
http://www.ars.usda.gov/is/kids/
This website includes great information on science projects and careers in agriculture.

USDA: Backyard Conservation
http://www.nrcs.usda.gov/wps/portal/nrcs/detail/national/newsroom/?cid=nrcs143_023574
This helpful site shows how to use agricultural conservation practices around the home.

Index

Photo Acknowledgments

The images in this book are used with the permission of: © XiXinXing/iStockphoto, 4; © MonkeyBusinessImages/iStockphoto, 5; © narvikk/iStockphoto, 6; © scotto72/iStockphoto, 7; © alexandrumagurean/iStockphoto, 8; © cjp/iStockphoto, 9; © Adwo/Shutterstock Images, 10; © oticki/iStockphoto, 11; © Rainer Lesniewski/Shutterstock Images, 12; © alle/iStockphoto, 13; © StoykoSabotanov/iStockphoto, 14; © Photo Image/Shutterstock Images, 15; © Gonzalo1978/iStockphoto, 16; © Fertnig/iStockphoto, 17; © Global Pics/iStockphoto, 18; © fotokostic/iStockphoto, 19; © clintscholz/iStockphoto, 20; © Simone-/iStockphoto, 21; © Dhoxax/iStockphoto, 22; © Tramino/iStockphoto, 23; © Ton Koene/VWPics/Newscom, 24; © defun/iStockphoto, 25; © Evgeny Sergeev/iStockphoto, 26; © gmcoop/iStockphoto, 27; Red Line Editorial, 28; © Pi-Lens/iStockphoto, 29; © northlightimages/iStockphoto, 30; © SVPhilon/Shutterstock Images, 31; © Envision/Corbis, 32; © Volodymyr Kyrylyuk/iStockphoto, 33; © Gianluca Figliola Fantini/iStockphoto, 34; © SolStock/iStockphoto, 35; © Cathy Yeulet/iStockphoto, 36; © skynesher/iStockphoto, 37.

Front Cover: © iStockphoto.com/northlightimages.

Main body text set in Adrianna Regular 14/20.
Typeface provided by Chank.

Searchlight
BOOKS™

What Can
We Do about
Pollution?

How Can We Reduce

Agricultural Pollution?

L. E. Carmichael

Lerner Publications ◆ Minneapolis

Content Consultant: Steven Cliff, Research Professor, Air Quality Research Center, University of California, Davis

Lerner Publications Company
A division of Lerner Publishing Group, Inc.
241 First Avenue North
Minneapolis, MN 55401 USA

For reading levels and more information, look up this title at
www.lernerbooks.com.

Library of Congress Cataloging-in-Publication Data

Carmichael, L. E. (Lindsey E.), author.
  How can we reduce agricultural pollution? / by L. E. Carmichael.
      pages cm. — (Searchlight books. What can we do about pollution?)
  Includes bibliographical references and index.
  ISBN 978-1-4677-9514-2 (lb : alk. paper) — ISBN 978-1-4677-9697-2 (pb : alk. paper)
— ISBN 978-1-4677-9698-9 (eb pdf) 1. Agricultural pollution—Juvenile literature. 2.
Agriculture—Environmental aspects—Juvenile literature. 3. Pollution prevention—
Juvenile literature. I. Title.
  TD195.A34C37 2016
  363.73'7—dc23

                                    2015032757

Manufactured in the United States of America
3-43052-20627-10/18/2016